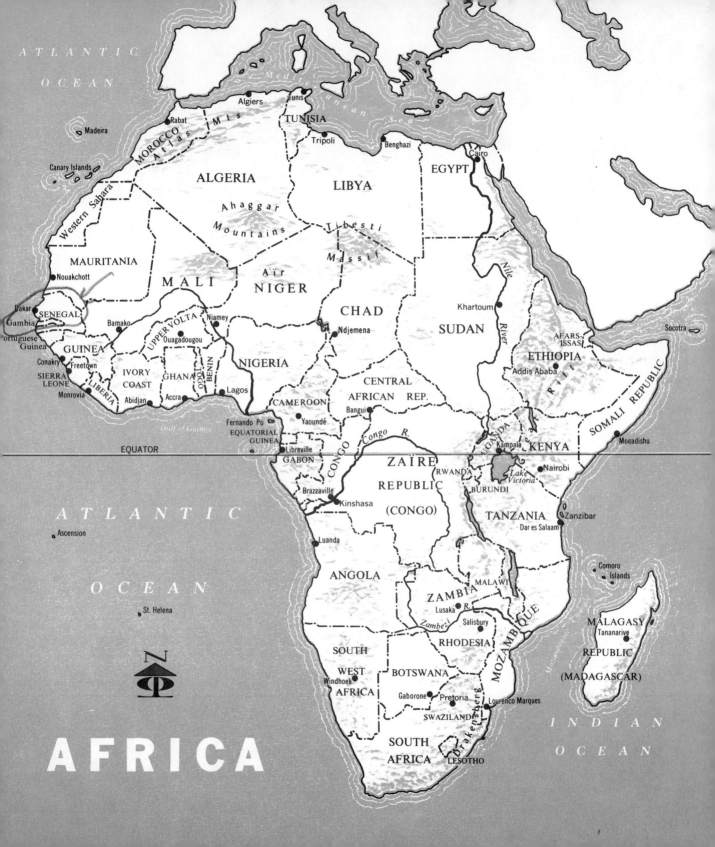

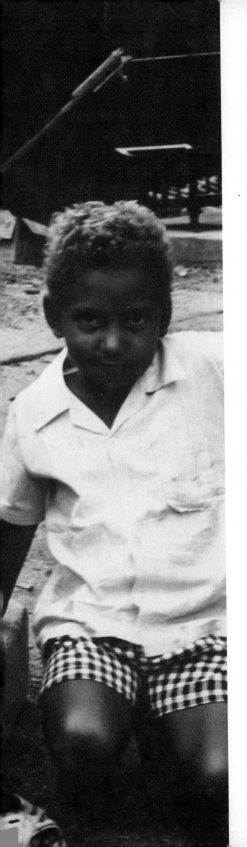

THE GAMBIA

by Allan Carpenter,
Loyd Kepferle,
and Susan Kepferle

Consulting Editor
Charles Berberich
Department of History
Northwestern University
Evanston, Illinois

 CHILDRENS PRESS, CHICAGO

THE ENCHANTMENT OF AFRICA

Available now: Benin, Botswana, Burundi, Cameroon, Central African Republic, Chad, Congo (Brazzaville), Egypt, Gambia, Gabon, Ghana, Ivory Coast, Kenya, Lesotho, Liberia, Libya, Malagasy Republic (Madagascar), Malawi, Mali, Mauritania, Morocco, Niger, Rhodesia, Rwanda, Senegal, Sierra Leone, Sudan, Swaziland, Tanzania, Togo, Tunisia, Uganda, Upper Volta, Zaïre Republic (Congo Kinshasa), Zambia

Planned for the future: Algeria, Equatorial Guinea, Ethiopia, Nigeria, Somali Republic, South Africa

ACKNOWLEDGMENTS

M.D. N'Jie, Information Office, The Republic of the Gambia, Banjul; Bakary Sidibe, Public Records Office, The Republic of the Gambia, Banjul; Embassy of the United States of America, Banjul; Embassy of Great Britain, Washington, D.C.

Cover Photograph: Mother and child, Allan Carpenter
Frontispiece: Gambian children, Michael Roberts

Project Editor: Joan Downing
Assistant Editor: Mary Reidy
Manuscript Editor: Janis Fortman
Map Artist: Eugene Dardeyn

LIBRARY OF CONGRESS
CATALOGING IN PUBLICATION DATA

Carpenter, John Allan, 1917-
    The Gambia.
    (Enchantment of Africa)

    SUMMARY: Introduces the geography, history, government, culture, and people of the small independent country in west Africa on the banks of the Gambia River.
    1. Gambia—Juvenile literature. [1. Gambia]
I. Kepferle, Loyd, joint author. II Kepferle, Susan, joint author. III. Title.
DT509.C37   966'.51   76-52910
ISBN 0-516-04564-4

Contents

A True Story to Set the Scene

TIRAMANG, FOUNDER OF AN EMPIRE

Sundiata (the emperor of the great Mali kingdom in the thirteenth century) received word that south of the Gambia River were fertile lands ruled by women. Sundiata decided to lead an army in hopes of conquering the land that is now the country of Senegal and adding it to his empire. But Tiramang, a general in Sundiata's army, wanted to lead the army for Sundiata. Tiramang told Sundiata: "You should not let hot food burn your hands when you have a spoon," meaning that Sundiata should let Tiramang take the risk. Tiramang wanted to lead the army so badly that he threatened to commit suicide if he was not allowed. Sundiata finally relented, and Tiramang left with an army of ninety thousand men.

Tiramang overcame the tribes already established in the lands to the south and became overlord of the new empire. He had his own *griots,* men who sang songs of praise and sang stories of Tiramang's brave feats to the accompaniment of their *koras,* or stringed instruments. Tiramang divided his empire, each division having its own government and *mansa,* or king, who paid homage and taxes to Tiramang.

Tiramang organized his empire so well that it lasted more than five hundred years. As a warrior, he instilled in his followers and descendants a love of battle and a love of the simple life, respect for courage, and the recognition that love of wealth only breeds corruption.

Groits *sing songs to the accompaniment of their* koras.

Rivers and creeks are Gambia's chief means of transportation.

8

The Face of the Land

The country of Gambia is a narrow strip of land along both sides of the Gambia River. The official name of the country is The Gambia. The smallest independent nation in Africa, Gambia varies from ten to forty miles in width. The country fol-

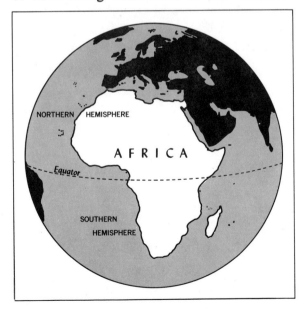

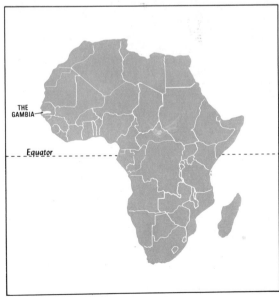

9

lows the Gambia River two hundred miles upstream from the Atlantic Ocean, and the capital, Banjul, is located at the mouth of the river.

Until recently, the river was the only means of transportation to the interior; now roads follow the river on both the north and south banks. The river, however, is still the chief means of transporting goods and people. Crops are sailed down the river in large, decorated canoes and in modern transports. The famous *Lady Wright,* a large steamer, plies the river once a week carrying people and an assortment of cargo: mail, cattle, rice, vegetables, chickens, and manufactured goods, along with farmers, traders, tourists, and schoolchildren (who travel free).

The river divides not only Gambia, but also the country of Senegal, which surrounds Gambia. There are nine ferry crossings along the river. This provides a steady stream of traffic between northern and southern Senegal. This crossing is crucial for the Senegalese, as it is the most direct route to Dakar from the Casamance (southern Senegal), which is referred to as the "breadbasket of Senegal." Gambia and Senegal are presently planning to build a bridge crossing the river.

The mouth of the Gambia River is one of the best natural harbors in Africa; a natural tidal action keeps it free of silt. Oceangoing vessels can navigate the river for 150 miles to Kuntaur, and smaller steamers can sail 50 miles farther.

The river determines where crops can be planted. The lower river, with its many estuaries, has dense mangrove swamps; consequently, there is little planting here, except in higher areas. Upriver, the swamps thin out, revealing a sandstone plateau, where crops can be grown close to the river. In the past, there was little irrigation from the river because tides carry saltwater more than one hundred miles upstream. The government plans to use the river for irrigation.

THE CLIMATE

Gambia has pleasant weather seven months of the year—a fact that attracts thousands of tourists. Beginning in November, the *harmattan,* a dry wind that blows southwesterly from the Sahara, brings temperatures in the eighties during the day and the low sixties at night. By December, mornings are cool. In April, the winds become light and variable, and the days and nights become hotter and much more humid; Gambians sit out at

MAP KEY

Albreda, E-2

Banjul, D-1
Bansang, D-5
Barra, D-1
Basse Santa Su, E-6
Brikama, E-1

Faraba Banta, E-1
Farafenni, D-3

Gambia River, D-1
D-2, D-3, D-4,

D-5, D-6, E-1,
E-2, E-5, E-6
Georgetown, D-5
Gunjur, E-1

Kerewan, D-2
Kombo, E-1
Kuntaur, D-5

MacCarthy Island, D-5

Serrekunda, D-1

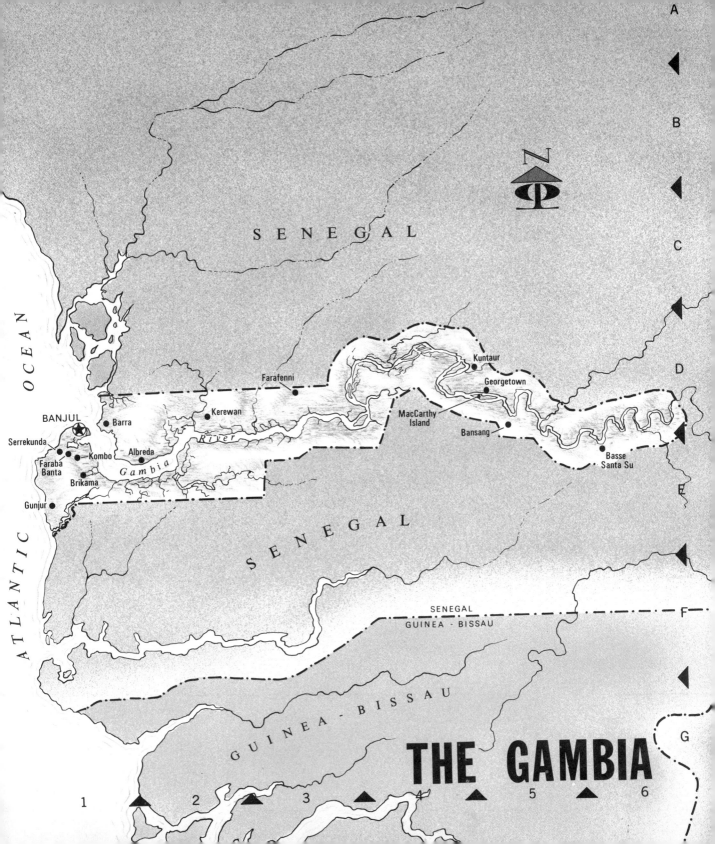

Above: The Lady Wright *docked at Banjul. Below: A ferry takes on passengers and cargo before crossing the river.*

night or, if they live near the ocean, go to the beach for relief from the cool breeze.

In June, after several afternoons of lightning and thunder, the rains finally begin. The sky opens and drops splatter. With the first drop, everyone leaves work to feel the rain. People are joyous: it is the first rain to fall in the country in eight or nine months. Children take off their clothes and run and splash in the puddles, people put out pans to catch the fresh water, and everyone dances and sings.

By the end of the first week of rains, planting has been completed. The leaves and grass are green, roads are muddy, and everyone talks about how the all-important peanut, rice, and *coos* (sorghum) crops are doing. During the summer, rain falls almost every day—often reaching forty-five inches. Sometimes the rain is so heavy that rivers run in the streets and children must stay home from school. But the rain does not usually last long. Soon the sun comes out, drying everything.

By the end of August, the rains have diminished. During the next two months,

The rains finally begin in June.

The bantaba tree (above) is like a giant shade tree while the baobab tree (below) looks as if its roots are growing upside down.

the heat and humidity become oppressive; this is a time when rich Gambians take vacations and farmers harvest their crops. In November the harmattan blows, and the cycle begins again.

Gambia's climate and vegetation do not reach the extremes of those in surrounding Senegal. In northern Senegal, where there is little undergrowth or trees, the weather is much drier and hotter in the daytime. In southern Senegal, trees and undergrowth become thicker and the rainfall is heavier; here the dense forests begin. In between, savanna covers Gambia—thick grass, some undergrowth, scrub trees and palms, and gigantic baobab and cottonwood trees. Gambia is low and flat, with no mountains—only a few very low hills. The highest point in the country is just 120 feet above sea level.

Three Children of The Gambia

LIZZIE OF BANJUL

Lizzie lives in Banjul in a *compound*—a fenced yard that surrounds five other houses besides her own. It is always noisy in the compound during the daytime: babies cry, visitors come and go, fish sellers call out, and radios blare. But Lizzie has lived here all her life and is used to the noises. She thinks of the other families in the compound almost as relatives.

Although Lizzie is a Roman Catholic, most of her schoolmates are Muslims. Lizzie attends a Catholic primary school, where she is in Standard Six (sixth grade). She has already taken the Common Entrance Examination, which determines whether she will continue on to high

Sometimes Lizzie's family goes to see a movie on Saturday night.

school, the four-year junior secondary school, or no school at all. Because she did very well on the test, space has been reserved for her at one of the four high schools in the country for the following

year. Since more children are attending primary school each year, there is not enough room for all to continue their education. Lizzie feels fortunate because she has been accepted into high school. She hopes to go to the university and become a teacher.

After school Lizzie goes home for dinner; then she usually goes back to school to study until six o'clock.

Lizzie's father works for the government, and her mother is a teacher. Her father was also a teacher for many years, and many of his students are now government officials or teachers. He is very active in Boy Scouts and is a troop leader.

Bcause Lizzie's father works for the government, he was able to get a car loan. He owns two houses, which he rents, and is saving money so that he can send his children to the university. Lizzie's older sister works as a secretary in an accounting office, her older brother is in high school and hopes to study abroad, and her younger brother spends much of his time playing soccer.

Lizzie thinks Banjul is the most exciting place in the country. Because her parents are very strict, Lizzie is not allowed to go out alone or to do some of the things she would like to do, yet she is still very active. She is a member of the Girl Guides, goes to movies and school picnics at the beach, and always goes to the circus and to special shows that come to town.

On Saturday, Lizzie helps her mother with the housecleaning and marketing. A Jola woman, who is a neighbor, does the wash and also helps with the housecleaning. Lizzie's mother has a refrigerator, and she does the cooking on an open fire.

On Saturday afternoons, Lizzie and her friends sometimes buy ice cream cones, which they eat at the beach, or they go to the parade ground, where they watch a soccer game. On Saturday nights, the family often goes to a movie. After church on Sunday, Lizzie and her family go visiting or have a picnic at the beach. Twice a year, their Senegalese relatives visit, and Lizzie practices her French with them. Although her relatives are Wolof, as is Lizzie, they speak mostly French in Dakar, where they live. Lizzie's family usually speaks Wolof at home, although they also speak English.

SEKOU OF FARABA BANTA

Sekou is a member of the Mandingo group, the largest group in Gambia. He lives in Faraba Banta, a quiet place overshadowed by spreading baobab and cottonwood trees. Except for a few shopkeepers and tailors, all the villagers are farmers, who plant peanuts and rice.

Sekou is twelve years old and in Standard Five (fifth grade). He is the first person in his family to go to school. During his first year of school, he learned English, which neither he nor his schoolmates knew. Now Sekou speaks English fairly well, although he has little chance to practice it outside of school because the villagers do not speak it.

Sekou also learns about the Koran (the

Sekou and his mother go to the market in Banjul to sell their mangoes.

holy book of the Islam religion) in a class at the mosque. In the past, Muslims felt that any other kind of teaching was inferior to their education. But the government has explained to the people that everyone can do better knowing how to read and write in English. Many of Sekou's people visited the big towns and saw that educated people get better jobs. So now all the boys, and some of the girls, in Faraba Banta go to school.

Sekou's older sister, who is fourteen, did not go to school because their father believed education was wrong for girls. He told her that there was no need for a farm girl and future wife (she will probably marry in about two years) to learn about foreign things. But next year, Sekou's younger sister will be going to school, although her father is still not convinced that she should.

Sekou's father works as a guard at an office building in Banjul. He is only home several weekends a month and for two weeks' vacation during the harvest season. As many other Gambians have done, Sekou's father went to the city so he could earn more money. Sekou's mother and older sister take care of the farming, and Sekou helps when he is out of school.

Sekou's favorite fruit is the mango, which is sweet and juicy, somewhat like a peach. When the mangoes are ripe, Sekou and his mother ride to Banjul in a taxi, bringing a big sack of the yellowish-red fruit to sell at the market. Sometimes

Sekou stays with his father in Banjul for several weeks. Sekou has made friends with some of the boys who play in the street outside of his father's office building. Sekou likes Banjul and wishes he could visit there more often. His favorite sight is the ferry landing; he likes to sit by the dock, watching the people load produce and cattle onto the ferry.

Sekou's mother works hard on the farm, and she has asked Sekou's father to marry a second wife to help her with her duties. Since Sekou's father has enough money, he will soon marry a fourteen-year-old relative.

If Sekou studies hard, he will probably have a chance to attend junior secondary school in Brikama, the nearest big town, in a few years. He thinks he would like to work in Banjul when he finishes school, but Sekou's father hopes Sekou will learn a trade first. Since the government is emphasizing the learning of modern farming techniques, Sekou could go to an agricultural school and return to farm his family's land.

MUSA OF FARAFENNI

Musa and his father are cattle herders. Sometimes they travel far upriver from their home village near Farafenni for three weeks at a time, trying to find good grazing for their cows. Musa's ancestors of the Fula group were herders as far back as the village elder's stories go. Musa's father is also a good storyteller. Musa has heard from him many old Fula stories of warriors and shepherds and the semidesert lands in the north, from which his great-grandparents originally came.

Musa's mother and three sisters live with his grandparents, and his uncle, aunt, and cousins live nearby. His aunt grows cotton, which his uncle weaves into cloth. The cloth is made of black, red, and white thread. Because the cloth is so beautiful, it is used for wedding skirts by the neighboring Fulas.

Musa would rather be with his father than stay home. Sometimes he and his father hunt birds and deer on their travels and bring the meat home for Musa's mother to prepare. Musa is a good shot with his father's gun, but he also knows how to kill birds with the slingshot he made. Musa's family is not rich, but with the whole family working, there is always enough to eat.

Recently, Musa's grandfather bought a radio. Now each evening, the whole family sits around it, listening to music and the news in the Fula language.

Musa's family is Muslim, and Musa knows how to write prayers in Arabic; he has memorized all the prayers his father says. Though some of his cousins go to school in the next village, Musa does not go. But Musa knows that an education is important, and he likes to listen to his cousins read.

When the school principal sees Musa's

Sekou likes to watch the ships and ferries at the port of Banjul.

father, he always asks when Musa is coming to school. Musa's father always gives the same reply—that there is no money for school fees and a uniform. But this is not the real reason. Musa's father does not want to change the traditional way of life. He does not want Musa to leave herding, which he feels is a good life and the only life for the family. Musa's father is afraid that if Musa goes to school, he might want to leave for the towns. Then perhaps Musa would feel that herding is not enough to satisfy him.

But Musa is happy herding the cattle with his father, and he does not want to go to school. Musa says that he will never go to school and never let his children go. But perhaps his attitude will change.

Musa is happy herding cattle and does not want to go to school.

MICHAEL ROBERTS

The Gambia Yesterday

For a long time, Americans and Europeans thought West Africa was a dark, uncivilized continent made up of isolated peoples who had no communication with each other. Actually, great empires and fine cities flourished in West Africa at many times. There was a great amount of movement among villages, groups, and even races. Migrations, strong leaders, religion, and trade combined to make West Africa a vital, politically organized area.

This was especially true of the area of present-day Gambia. Various groups migrated here throughout the years, bringing their beliefs and customs and changing them to fit the area. Highly organized states, ruled by kings and subkings, existed for hundreds of years on both sides of the Gambia River. Traders from as far away

as the Arab countries made their way to the mouth of this river.

EARLY HISTORY

Little is known about Gambia's earliest inhabitants. But the main groups today —the Wolof, Mandingo, Soninke, and Fula—are said to have migrated to the Gambia River valley from other sections of West Africa many centuries ago.

Prior to the twelfth century A.D., about twelve large stone circles were built along the banks of the upper Gambia River. These circles range from ten to fifteen feet in diameter, with stones from three to nine feet high. Because artifacts and bones have been dug up at the sites, the stones probably surrounded the graves of chiefs.

A sailing ship used in the fourteenth century.

Archaeologists believe that the stones were put in the earth by the Jola, a group still in existence in Gambia and Senegal.

THE GHANA EMPIRE

Gambia was on the edge of several powerful empires. By 1000 A.D., the Ghana empire extended from the Gambia River on the south to the Sahara on the north. The center of Ghana's power, in what is now southeast Mauritania, commanded the southern end of the caravan routes that traveled through the Sahara and to the Arab countries.

The present areas of Gambia, Senegal, Mali, and Guinea were once vassal states of the Soninke clan, who ruled the Ghana empire. Although the exact origin of the empire is not known, it existed "at least twenty-two kings before the Hegira." (The Hegira is Muhammed's flight from Mecca in 622.) According to an Arab explorer, the king of the empire was "the wealthiest of all kings on the face of the earth on account of the riches he owned and the hoards of gold acquired by him . . ." In the army of the empire were two hundred thousand foot soldiers and forty thousand archers and cavalrymen.

Kumbi Saleh, the capital city of the empire, was actually two towns. The emperor and local people lived in one town, while visiting Muslim traders lived in the other.

During the eleventh century, Berber groups led by fanatical Muslims from North Africa, called the Almoravids, invaded the Ghana empire, converting some of the local people to Islam. The already weak Ghana empire was soon taken over by the Almoravids, but they ruled for only a short time. After about 1100, the Soninke people of Ghana regained their independence, and a number of their states flourished until the rise of the Mali empire (in the 1230s). The greatest of these successors to Ghana was the Susu state of Kaniaga.

During the period of the Ghana empire (about 500 to 1200), various peoples moved into the Gambia River valley. Traders from as far east as Sudan reached the mouth of the Gambia River.

THE MALI EMPIRE

The Mandingo peoples originally came from Manding, near the source of the Gambia River in the mountains of Guinea. They settled in many parts of West Africa, but mostly at the bend of the Niger River. During the ninth century, Mali, the Mandingo empire, was a small state. During the next three hundred years, it was part of the Ghana empire, then the Susu empire.

It is said that the Susu emperor, Sumanguru, killed eleven sons of the king of the Mandingo. But he spared the king's crippled son, Sundiata, because he thought the boy was harmless. When Sundiata recovered from his lameness, he overthrew Sumanguru and became known as one of Africa's greatest leaders. In 1240 Sundiata subdued what was left of the Ghana empire, took over the neighboring

A Mandingo chief talks to a village leader.

Above: The writing on this boat shows the Arabic influence in Gambia. Below: Cadamosto was attacked on his first visit to Gambia.

kingdoms, and founded an organization of allied states under his control. During his twenty-five-year rule, Sundiata extended his boundaries and encouraged trade and agriculture.

According to stories told in Gambia and Senegal, one of Sundiata's generals, Tiramang, was sent to the area south of the Gambia River, where a few Mandingos had settled. Tiramang left with an army of ninety thousand men. He added conquered Jola, Fula, and Bainounka groups to his army. Tiramang was set up as mansa of this area, which was called Kaabu. He immediately divided the land into separate states, each with its own subking reporting to Tiramang and ultimately to the emperor, Sundiata.

After Sundiata died, the empire was ruled by members outside the family. It was Mansa Musa, Sundiata's grandson, who fifty years later caused the name of the Mali empire to be added to the chronicles of the Arab scholars. After extending the boundaries of the Mali empire, in 1324 he made a pilgrimage to Mecca by way of Cairo, showing everyone his immense wealth. According to an Egyptian scribe, Mansa Musa took "sixty thousand men with him, including twelve thousand slaves dressed in silks and brocades. Five hundred slaves each carried a staff of gold and in a baggage train of eighty camels, each carried three hundred pounds of gold dust." It was said he distributed twenty thousand pieces of gold as alms.

A devout Muslim, Mansa Musa created the famed Islamic center in Timbuktu. That university became a center of learning for the Arab and African world. After Mansa Musa died, the empire was weakened by family fights. By 1400 the Mali empire ruled only a small area. But Kaabu, the area south of the Gambia River, continued to be dominated by Mandingo kings until the 1800s.

The people of Kaabu were farmers, and their chief crops were rice, millet, and cotton. Cotton cloth was used as currency. Mandingo traders, or *dyulas,* were highly successful. It is said that Momadi Konte, a dyula, had so many slaves that his cotton could be picked, spun, and woven all in one day.

The mansas, who were warrior rulers, taxed their people. Fula herders paid in livestock, and traders paid in cotton. The rest of the people paid in cloth, millet, livestock, and slaves. The mansas were forbidden to do any farm work and also forbidden to collect great wealth. All the taxes were spent on themselves and their extended families, yet there never seemed to be enough to meet all the needs.

PORTUGUESE TRADERS

Alvise Cadamosto was a Venitian explorer employed by Prince Henry of Portugal. He arrived at the mouth of the Gambia River in search of gold and ivory. Though his ship was turned away by armed canoeists, he returned the following year. After Cadamosto, Portuguese traders came regularly to the area.

The Portuguese traded beads, guns, horses, and cloth for beeswax, gum, pepper, ivory, slaves, and gold. Very soon after they arrived, the Portuguese were trading for slaves to take to Portugal and Brazil. At first, slaves were brought from lands as far away as the Sudan and Mali through Senegal and to Albreda and James Island. Later, local Gambian chiefs sold slaves captured in tribal conflicts. By the end of the eighteenth century, four thousand slaves a year were being sent across the Atlantic from Gambia, and traders were receiving about two hundred dollars each for healthy young men.

Despite their cultural influence, the Portuguese were never able to win in war against the peoples of Gambia or neighboring Senegal. The strong kingdoms of the Wolofs in Senegal and the Mandingos in Gambia successfully resisted European influence for many years. At times, great leaders rose among them, combining the states into large empires. Biram Jenne Kumba, a Wolof, reigned over the area between the Gambia and Senegal rivers. In 1512 a Fula leader named Koli defeated the Wolofs, and later their country split into a number of smaller states. Koli conquered the whole Senegal Valley and crossed the Gambia River several times with his army. Koli's descendants ruled inland, while the Wolof controlled the coast and the Mandingo mansas ruled Gambia.

Though the Portuguese remained in Gambia for only a short time, they influenced the area greatly. Portuguese traders brought the peanut (now Gambia's principal crop) from Brazil; they also

The Portuguese taught the Gambians how to make their fishing canoes.

INFORMATION OFFICE, THE REPUBLIC OF GAMBIA

brought orange, lime, and papaya trees. Because they were fishermen, they taught the Gambians how to make the Portuguese fishing canoe. This type of brightly colored canoe is still used in Gambia.

Missionaries came with the traders, establishing small settlements on the river. Many Portuguese married Mandingo women, and their children were called *mulattoes*. A powerful mulatto trading class developed and existed long after the Portuguese left in the sixteenth century. The Portuguese-Mandingo mulattoes influenced the whole area by copying the Portuguese style of house, planting shade trees in yards, and establishing Portuguese-Creole as the speech of all trading on the river.

By 1500 the Songhai empire had taken over much of the Mali empire. The Mandingo kingdom south of the Gambia River remained part of the Mali empire. Though the Wolof on the north bank had a strong kingdom, they were paying tribute to emperors of the Songhai empire.

BRITISH EXPLORATION

The Portuguese lost interest in Gambia because lands to the south seemed richer. The hoped-for gold and ivory only existed in small amounts. Consequently, in 1588 the Portuguese sold their rights on the Gambia River to the British.

Immediately, British traders began sailing into the Gambia River. In 1618 British explorer George Thompson traveled far up the Gambia River, believing it was a branch of the Niger River that could be navigated to the fabulous cities of Gao and Timbuktu. Since he could find no connection between the two rivers, Thompson gave up his exploration and began trading with local people. Captain Richard Jobson came up the Gambia River in 1620 with two ships and traded for gold and ivory. He was met by a rich local trader, who visited the ships with musicians and two hundred followers, not allowing anyone but himself to trade with the foreigners.

By 1660 the British had established the Company of Royal Adventurers on a small island twenty miles up the river. Slaves were the primary interest of the traders at this time, although the company charter stated that the trade for gold, pepper, and elephants' teeth was the purpose of forming the company.

For a time, the Company of Royal Adventurers controlled the slave trade. It made arrangements to supply a certain number of slaves to West Indies planters each year in return for sugar. In 1672 the Royal Africa Company replaced the Company of Royal Adventurers. The Dutch arrived in Gambia to trade, attacking the company's ships and trading stations. But the British soon regained command.

During the next hundred years, both the French and British claimed the Gambia River. The British built James Island into a fort complete with bastions, towers, army barracks, and slave quarters. From 1665 the British Crown supported the fort. The French settled in a village called Albreda, directly across from the fort, and made

A drawing of James Island as it looked in 1732.

treaties with local tribes. The French attacked and captured Fort James four different times, but the British always regained command. Because the fort was in the middle of the river, it was in command of all ships trying to pass. It forced all foreign vessels to pay a duty of 10 percent on all goods.

About 1667 there was a slave revolt. Slaves being held on the island revolted, killing all but one of the thirty-two Englishmen at the fort. Unfortunately for the slaves, a British ship arrived and quickly recaptured the island, killing more than forty of the slaves, who had been unable to escape to the mainland.

Often the English and French were at the mercy of the Mandingo mansas, because all of the firewood and fresh water of James Island had to be bought from them. At the mouth of the river the power of the Europeans and Gambians was well balanced. The farther upriver the Europeans went, the more the Gambians were able to make them act as the guests of a country should.

SETTLEMENT

Britain had given British merchants trade rights to the Gambia River in 1588, and British soldiers had defended the river from foreign merchants. But Britain had not held any Gambian land except as trading territory. The fort on the tiny James Island was Britain's oldest settlement in West Africa, but it had been abandoned by 1800.

In the 1783 Treaty of Versailles, Gambia was given to Britain, and France retained only the town of Albreda. Neither France nor Britain worried about giving away land that they did not own. But no one had consulted the rulers of the Gambian kingdoms or their people. Naturally, Gambians became quite upset when British governors came to tell them what to do.

In 1807 Britain abolished slave trading. Gambia was officially declared a Settlement and was put under the jurisdiction of the British in Sierra Leone—four hundred miles away. British traders, their wives, and Wolof who were friendly with the British settled in Gambia. But there was not enough living space for all these people, so the British pushed for more land. Britain purchased the island of Banjul (on the south bank of the mouth of the river) in 1916, from the chief of Kombo, the kingdom in that area. The purchase of Banjul (called Bathurst by the British until 1973) marks the beginning of colonialism in Gambia.

The British built a military post on Banjul—then a swampy island, dense with mangrove trees. The island was divided into a number of villages, each with land

A drawing of Fort Louvel, Banjul, in 1831.

Government House on MacCarthy Island. The large trees are growing on the site of the old fort and barracks.

for pasture and cultivation. Each village was for a separate group—Wolof Town for Senegalese emigrants, Soldier Town for retired soldiers, Jola Town for people of the Jola clan, and Portuguese Town for Portuguese settlers. The town of Bathurst was for European merchants, wealthy Gambian merchants, and wealthy mulattoes. Eventually the separate sections merged. But even today, the island is divided into the same sections; in many cases, descendants of the original inhabitants still live in the same areas.

The Settlement grew steadily as the British signed more treaties with Gambian chiefs. In 1826 the British bought the land across the river. This area became known as the "Ceded Mile" because it was one mile wide and thirty-six miles long.

LIBERATED SLAVES

In 1831, freed slaves from the British West Indies in the Caribbean were sent to Sierra Leone and then on to Gambia. When they first arrived, they were sent far upriver to MacCarthy Island to farm. The freed slaves were poor and not used to Africa. Most of the liberated slaves had been born in the New World, so they did not speak the local languages or understand the people. They brought with them Western dress, Western education, and the Christian religion.

THE CREATION OF A COLONY

During the middle 1800s, there were political and religious wars in Gambia.

34

Gambians were also disturbed by the presence of the English and the liberated slaves.

Kementang, the king of Upper Niani (a kingdom inland on the north bank), waged war in the area around MacCarthy Island in 1831, taking slaves. The people on the island organized an army, and soldiers were sent from Bathurst, forcing Kementang to withdraw.

That same year, the king of Barra (a kingdom on the north bank at the mouth of the river) attacked the British at Barra Point. Soldiers escaped across the river to Bathurst. Finally, because Gambian allies were not interested in helping, the governors in Senegal and Sierra Leone sent help. After several months of skirmishes, peace was declared and another treaty was signed to honor the "Ceded Mile." But Kementang again attacked MacCarthy Island, in 1834, and burned the Government House and houses of the liberated slaves.

In 1843 Gambia was chartered as a separate colony, with its own governor. Temporary peace came to Gambia and the colony began to export peanuts. By 1848 the value of peanuts exported was about two hundred fifty thousand dollars.

In 1857 the last French outpost in Gambia, the trading town of Albreda, was sold to Great Britain.

As years passed, the Kaabu empire slowly weakened because of lax rule and quarrels among the rulers. Other groups grew in strength. After a combined Soninke-Fula attack in 1868, the empire

fell—never to return to its former glory.

SONINKI-MARABOUT WARS

In the mid-nineteenth century, a growing group of orthodox Muslims became a powerful force and revolted against the traditional rulers. For fifty years, the area of the Gambia River was torn by conflicts. Traders had become deeply religious Muslims throughout the years because of their close relationship with Muslims from the north and east. Members of noble families had accepted most Muslim beliefs, but not all—for example, they drank alcoholic beverages, which was against Koranic law. The trading class and their spiritual followers were called *marabouts,* and their opponents from the nobility were called *soninki.* The soninki did not follow all the practices of Islam.

There was no clear victory for either the soninki or the marabouts. The result of the wars was that Gambia became more Islamized. But the religious reformers did not agree among themselves, and their political disunity allowed the British to take over Gambia's political organization.

From 1866 to 1888, the Settlement of The Gambia (made up of Banjul, part of Kombo, and the "Ceded Mile") had its own legislative body but was again administratively part of Sierra Leone. In 1888 it was made a separate colony with its own administrative, executive, and legislative council. In 1889 England and France agreed on boundaries for Gambia.

Gambia Today

The French began taking an interest in the upper river, so the area outside the Colony of Bathurst was formed into a protectorate with seventeen districts. Each district was under a head chief and had native courts.

One section of the Gambia Valley was not under the protectorate—the land of a great Fula chief, Muls Molo. Muls Molo was originally pro-British, but he became disenchanted with the foreign intruders. He attacked the Portuguese in Bissau and the English in Gambia and tried to stir up the whole country against the British. Fodi Kabba and Fodi Silah also led the religious wars and turned against the British. Today Gambians sing songs about these great heroes and tell stories of their adventures.

Eventually, it became clear that Gambian leaders could not resist the British. Their armies could not defeat machine guns and steamboats. The kings of the Gambian states watched resentfully as district commissioners came to supervise the protectorate. In Bathurst a large group of Western-educated Gambians began to read and think about running their country themselves. The British brought some benefits, but they kept the Gambians out of the government and used the country's resources for their own purposes.

INDEPENDENCE

Stirrings of independence began as early as 1920, when Edward Francis Small gave up his study for the priesthood

President Jawara addressing a crowd in a village.

Voting registration in a rural area.

and decided to devote himself to helping Gambia. He founded the country's first newspaper in 1923. Six years later, he founded the Bathurst Trade Union, which brought the workers wage increases after an eighty-two-day strike.

In 1954 elections were held for the first time to bring Gambians into the legislature. Edward Small and Sheik Omar Fye (a businessman and a Muslim) were the first Gambian members of the Legislative Council.

At the time of Small's death in 1958, three political parties had developed. Their leaders were all ministers in the government. M. E. Jallow continued Small's work on the union.

DAWDA KAIRABA JAWARA

President Dawda Kairaba Jawara has gained the world's respect as an extremely able leader. He has encouraged modernization without borrowing huge sums of money.

Jawara came from a small Mandingo village. When he was young, he was taken to live with an uncle in Banjul, because education was lacking in the rural areas. His uncle sent him to school, where Jawara proved to be a brilliant student. One of the few Muslims to attend high school, he was awarded a scholarship to study veterinary medicine in Great Britain. Jawara was the chief veterinary officer for the government of Gambia when he entered politics.

FORMATION OF A REPUBLIC

Britain granted Gambia full internal self-government in 1963. P. S. Njie,

THE
GAMBIA

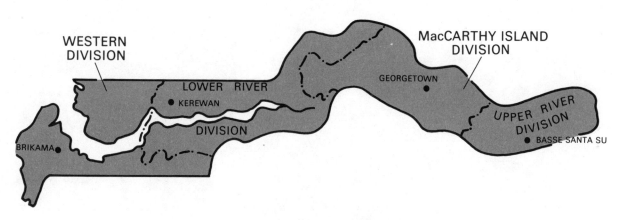

WESTERN
DIVISION

MacCARTHY ISLAND
DIVISION

LOWER   RIVER

GEORGETOWN

KEREWAN

DIVISION

UPPER RIVER
DIVISION

BRIKAMA

BASSE SANTA SU

GOVERNMENTAL
DIVISIONS

A street scene in Banjul. The building in the background is the Quadrangle where most of the government offices are.

40

leader of the United Party, was made chief minister by the British governor, but his party had not won the election. The winning party, the People's Progressive Party (PPP), led by Dawda Kairaba Jawara, was bypassed. So the PPP and the Democratic Congress Alliance (DCA) joined and asked for independence. A new constitution was prepared, and elections were held a year later. The PPP and DCA won, and Jawara became prime minister.

Jawara and the country prepared for independence. With much fanfare, Gambia achieved independence on February 18, 1965, becoming a "constitutional monarchy within the British Commonwealth of Nations." In 1970 the people voted to become a republic, and Jawara was elected president.

THE GOVERNMENT

The government is divided into three branches: executive, legislative, and judicial. The president is chief of state and head of the government. He is elected by the majority party to a five-year term. The vice-president is elected at the same time as the president and must be of the same political party.

The president selects his cabinet from the thirty-seven members of Parliament. The members of Parliament hold five-year terms of office: Thirty-two of the members are elected by popular vote, and four members are elected by the local chiefs. The attorney general, who is appointed by the president, automatically becomes a member of Parliament. In March of 1972, President Jawara's PPP won twenty-eight of the thirty-two seats in Parliament, the United Party won three seats, and an independent party won one.

The country is divided into six area councils containing the thirty-five traditional district councils. Each council has its own treasury. The local chiefs retain the traditional powers of law. Each village also has an official leader, called an *alcalhi,* who represents the village to local government and other bureaucrats.

Gambia is officially neutral; however, it is especially close to the United Kingdom, from which Gambia still receives aid and special trading favors. The United Nations accepted Gambia as its 115th member in September of 1965. Gambia is a member of the Organization of African States (OAS) and the Commonwealth of Nations.

VOTING PROCEDURE

Gambia's voting procedure is unique in Africa and is often considered to be the fairest method for a country with any illiterate voters. To be eligible to vote, one must obtain a voting card with a recent picture of the voter. On election day, the voter takes the card to the polling site, where it is exchanged for a voting marble. The voter enters a booth with several barrels—one for each political party. On each barrel is clearly shown the name of the party, its colors and emblem, and the name and picture of the party's candidate. The voter drops the marble into

Education is very important in Gambia and a large portion of the government's budget is used for improvements. Above: Children in an elementary school. Right: A classroom block of the Gambia High School. Below: A high school mathematics class.

Many Gambians are now going to technical schools. The skills they learn will help them find better employment. Left: An apprentice operating a lathe. Below: A trainee welder at work on a pile driver.

Oxen are usually used to plow the fields.

the barrel of his choice. When the election officials hear the marble drop, they cancel the voting card.

EDUCATION

The government places a high priority on education. Gambia's literacy rate has been estimated at 25 percent. While the country still has far to go before all Gambians can read and write, much has already been accomplished on the road toward literacy.

The first schools were run by missionaries. As early as 1821, there were two schools—one for boys and one for girls. Most students were children of liberated slaves, but others slowly became interested in education, too—especially in the Banjul area. In 1875 Boy's High School was started by the Methodist missionaries; forty years later, Girl's High School was opened. Until 1945, all Banjul schools were mission schools partially supported by the government.

Presently there are ninety-five primary schools, seventeen junior secondary schools (seventh to tenth grade, which are not as concerned with academic subjects as the high schools), four high schools, four technical schools, and a teacher training college. As there is no university in the country, the government provides scholarships for students to attend a university abroad—usually in Nigeria, Sierra Leone, Ghana, or the United Kingdom.

New technology has introduced tractors for plowing the fields.

Gambia's high schools are staffed by qualified college graduates; the junior secondary schools, however, do not have as well-qualified teachers. The Department of Education is trying to attract more highly educated people to teach in the elementary schools; at present, some of the teachers are not even high school graduates. The classes in the primary and junior secondary schools are overcrowded, with sometimes as many as forty or fifty students in a class.

A large problem in Gambia is how to cope with the large number of partially educated students who compete for places in the junior secondary schools and high schools, but who cannot enter because of lack of space. They are usually not content to go back to work in their home town or village. Most want to finish high school, travel or study abroad, and then enter government service. Yet there are not enough jobs available in the towns. These youths walk the streets of the towns, trying to get work, but only becoming a burden on their friends or relatives. The tourist business is a partial answer. In this business decent wages can be earned. But tourism cannot employ all of these youths. In his 1973 address President Jawara stated that the government hopes to attract youth to agriculture by upgrading farms, teaching modern technology, and showing examples of successful modern farmers.

Natural Treasures

ANIMALS

Different varieties of snakes are found in Gambia's swamps and forests, including the African python (which sometimes exceeds twenty feet), the fast-moving Smyth's water snake, and the extremely poisonous green mamba. The python, monitor lizard, and the crocodile are hunted for their skins, which are used to make bags and purses.

Birds are everywhere. Some, such as the guinea fowl, are hunted, while others are just photographed and recorded by bird-watchers. There are more than four hundred species of birds in Gambia; some, like the fish-storing pelican, crested crane, and secretary birds, are quite large; others are very tiny, such as the crimson Senegal fire-finch and the scarlet-breasted sun-bird. Many of the birds are brightly colored, and each serves a specific function. Some birds eat fish, some eat snakes, some eat rodents, and some eat rice. The hooded vulture and the pied crow are always present to pick up any scraps of food left untended. One variety of rice bird, the size of a robin, builds a nest in the cottonwood trees that is five feet wide. The weaverbird weaves an elaborate nest that looks like a long stocking turned upside down. The variety and color of Gambia's birds makes the country a bird-watcher's paradise.

When President Siaka Stevens of Sierra Leone visited Gambia in 1970, he was asked what he would like to take home with him. Without having to think about

The crested crane, one of the many birds in Gambia.

Opposite: Many kinds of fish can be caught at the Atlantic shore. Above: The tree in the center is called the beelzabub tree.

This man is collecting wine from the palm tree.

50

it, he answered, "Bonga fish." Boxes of the small and bony but succulent smoked fish were packed in the airplane when he left. Although Gambians prefer bonga, the country is rich in many kinds of fish. The most delicious-tasting ones are sole, ladyfish, shark, tuna, and barracuda.

Other sea life is also found in Gambia, including sixty-pound sea turtles, shrimp, lobster, eel, octopus, and clams. Porpoises play in Banjul's harbor.

Once game was plentiful in Gambia. Nineteenth-century colonialists described hartebeest, water buffalo, lions, elephants, and giraffes in their journals. But now, these are gone. Of the larger animals, red colobus, green monkeys, and great troops of baboons remain, as well as timid hippopotamuses, leopards, anteaters, hyenas, deer, and crocodiles. Because wild boar tear up the fields upriver and hippopotamuses love rice, the farmers consider these animals pests. The monitor lizard, often four or five feet long, is found throughout the country.

PLANTS

Without its leaves, the baobab tree is grotesque. East Africans say when God created the baobab tree, he made a mistake and put it in upside down—that what are seen are not branches but roots.

The giant baobab tree is a source of great pleasure to Gambians. Underneath its spreading branches, villagers build their houses. When it has leaves, the tree is beautiful and the large, gnarled trunk is magnificent. The pear-shaped fruit, as big as a coconut, hangs strangely from a two-foot stem. The inside of the fruit is like a fluffy, cotton ball and tastes a little like cotton candy. Children eat the insides raw, but the insides also make a sweet soup that is poured over rice. The leaves are also edible, and rope is made from the bark.

Other large trees grow in Gambia. Cottonwoods grow as large as the baobab, and *bantamas,* platforms on which the men of the village sit and gossip, are often placed beneath the branches of a cottonwood.

There are many coconut palms, rafia palms, and dum palms. The only evergreen is the large and graceful casuarina. The malina is a fast-growing tree imported from India; it is used for fence posts and house beams.

The forests of the south bank are rapidly disappearing as the farmers clear and burn them to allow room for peanut fields. Large trees still dot the landscape. Along the roads are tall, skinny palm trees with bunches of bottles tied around the crowns; these are used for collecting palm wine, a naturally fermented liquid that tastes like grape juice.

Most compounds, even those in town, have such fruit trees as mango, orange, lime, papaya, guava, and banana. Some people have begun to grow other fruit, such as pineapple and watermelon. Vegetables also grow well in Gambia. During different seasons, tomatoes, cabbage, lettuce, bitter balls, *eddo* (a type of potato), corn, cucumbers, potato greens, and hot peppers are plentiful.

The People Live in The Gambia

In Gambia, an extended family includes parents, children, uncles, aunts, cousins, half brothers, half sisters, great aunts, and great uncles. A Gambian might call someone "brother" who is really his second cousin, or he might call someone "uncle" who is really his grandfather's cousin.

In Gambia there are no orphans; there are no unwanted children. Children whose parents have died are usually raised by relatives. Many children live with people other than their parents, for reasons of education or preference. For example, Dawda Jawara, president of Gambia, did not live with his parents but with an uncle who offered to educate him.

Often a child is given to a friend or relative who has no children. The Mandingos often give their first child to the husband's mother, to comfort and help her in her old age. At the same time, old people are taken care of by relatives, usually with love and attention. It is the duty of a son or daughter to care for his parents when they can no longer care for themselves.

Although wealth is desirable, it is difficult to become wealthy in Gambia, since a person who has a good job is responsible for the other members of his extended family. If a cousin does not have rice today, his relatives share theirs; if a young man or woman wants to go to a foreign country to study, he or she borrows money from all his relatives and close friends. The prestige of the student will be reflected on all who helped send him to school. When the student returns to Gambia, he

Since homes have no running water, water is collected from public hydrants and carried home.

usually pays the money back by helping another relative who wants to study abroad.

As material goods are shared, food is also shared. A Gambian woman would not think of cooking just enough for her family—she always cooks extra for whomever may stop by when the family is ready to eat. A visitor who is a friend or neighbor eats from the common pot; an important visitor eats separately.

If a member of the family is lazy, there is no attempt to push the person out of the household. The family may make strong remarks or hints to get a job, but there is no attempt to force anyone out.

Ninety percent of all Gambians are Muslims; the other 10 percent are either Christians or animists, people who believe in spirits. The Muslims keep some of the animist beliefs, but also hold to the main Muslim rules: they believe there is no God but Allah and that Muhammed is his prophet; Muslims pray five times daily, facing east; they say the Friday noonday prayers; they give alms; they keep the fast of Ramadan; and, if financially possible, they make the pilgrimage, or *hadj,* to the holy city of Mecca (in Saudi Arabia).

Although it is not a part of the Islam religion, most Gambians wear *gri-gri,* a fetish or charm that has magical powers, as protection. In many cases, the gri-gri is simply paper with Arabic phrases written on it. The paper is enclosed in a leather pouch and hung around the neck, waist, or high on the arm, or sometimes worn in the hair.

Many Gambians believe that witches and devils have the power to put spells on

No one tries to push a lazy person out of the family group or household.

There are no unwanted children in Gambia.

Many Gambian women wear head ties made of the same pattern as their dresses.

people. When they get sick and believe that someone has put a spell on them, they go to a famous marabout, a herbalist, or a known sorcerer. These experts try to relieve the symptoms with medicine and prayer. A known worker of spells is always left alone—for nobody wants to incur his or her wrath.

CEREMONIES

A tradition held more than hundreds of years by the Wolof group is the naming ceremony. The naming ceremony is very important, especially for the first child. All friends, as well as important acquaintances, are invited to this ceremony.

As soon as the baby is born, a fire is started in the house. On the morning of the naming ceremony, exactly one week after birth, the fire is put out and the mother sweeps away the ashes. The child is washed with a special bath water that contains leaves, grass, bark, and a silver ring. The mother washes, too.

Visitors arrive and coins are given to the mother if the baby is a girl, to the father if the baby is a boy. Women shave the baby's head, and its hair is hidden in a special place so witches cannot get it and put a spell on the baby. An elder may say prayers over the child and rub his hands over its head; he spits in its ears to make sure the child's name is implanted.

The name of the child is told to the visitors, and prayers are said so the child will have prosperity and long life. If the family has enough money, an animal is slain and food is prepared. Kola nuts, a symbol of hospitality throughout West Africa, are handed out, as well as cakes made of rice flour.

Gambians love dancing and drumming. When a girl is getting married, her friends hold an *asherbi* dance. Asherbi means "wearing the same clothes": the girl's friends, who are of the same tribe, all buy cloth of the same design and have it made into dancing dresses and head ties. If the marriage is held in a town, the street is blocked off, rented chairs are put in a circle, and drummers are hired. To the beat of drums, the girls run in turn into the circle, dance several minutes, then run out. If people like a girl's dance or if the drumming is especially good, coins are thrown into the circle. Young men like to take their turns, too. As the drumming becomes faster later on in the dance, the dancers show off and the dancing becomes very lively.

If the dance is for a special occasion, such as the marriage of a very important couple, or if it is for a holiday or an important visitor, visitors and dancers dress in fancy clothes, perhaps expensive velvet dresses and fine jewelry.

FOOD

Gambians are very careful about how they cook their food. The staple food is rice. A soup or sauce is always prepared to pour over the rice. Because food is plentiful, there are many varieties of sauce and many different recipes. Although the main

Above: A young Wolof girl. Right: Women from the interior weave coins into their hair. Below: A Gambian trader's wife with braided hair and gold earrings.

afternoon dinner is rice, the evening meal (taken after prayers at sundown) is often coos covered with the sauce used at dinner. Rice is thought to be too heavy for evening, although it is eaten if coos is not available. Often a mush made of sugar, milk, and rice or coos is made for breakfast. In the rainy season, when lettuce is plentiful, salads are common.

A typical dinner is *domadah*—beef cooked with water, peanut butter, tomato sauce, hot pepper, and onions. The domadah is ladled on top of rice. People eat it with their hands or with a big spoon. For important visitors, the domadah is made with chicken.

Since fish is so plentiful along the coast, it is the most common dish there. *Sipa sipa* (shrimp), oysters, and clams are cooked the same way. Vegetables such as bitter balls, tomatoes, and cabbage are often added to the sauce. A luxurious dish that takes almost all day to prepare is fish balls.

THE PEOPLES

Jola Probably the longest residents of Gambia's south bank are the Jola. Although a small group in Gambia, most of them have refused to integrate with the other groups. During the last one hundred years, some have become Roman Catholics and a few have recently become Muslims through intermarriage, but most still remain animists.

The Jolas have never had a centralized government; there has never been a head chief. Instead, each village has always had its own chief. Jolas are known for their skill at farming, their big houses, and their clean villages.

Wolof The Wolof area is Banjul and the north bank of the river. When the Portuguese came, the Wolof ruled in Senegal in a group of highly organized kingdoms with strong chiefs. After about 1800, many Wolofs migrated from Senegal, and most Gambian Wolofs are descended from these immigrants. Today Gambian Wolofs have strong ties with Senegalese north of the river.

The Wolof are a tall and handsome people, who dress beautifully. They have been Muslims for hundreds of years. Today Wolof are often active in politics and education. They still have a rather strong caste system, although the educated people do not pay as much attention to it as before, especially regarding marriage. In the past, Wolof people were expected to marry within their own caste.

Mandingo The Mandingo are the largest ethnic group in Gambia, making up more than half the country's population. Mandingos migrated hundreds of years ago from the area east of Gambia. During the Mali empire, the groups were led by noblemen. To this day, there is still a noble class of Mandingos. Mainly farmers, Mandingos are often very tall. The women wear large gold earrings and carefully tied headscarves. The men wear a distinctive pleated type of pants; in the past, the width of a man's pants determined his status—wide pants meant he had received many honors.

Fula Fula people are still partly nomadic, as they were in the past, when they herded their cattle and sheep into Gambia from the north and east. It is possible that the Fula are a mixture of Senegalese clans and Saharan Berber groups. Fulas (or Fulani or Fulbe, as they are also known) live throughout West Africa in the drier regions, usually as herders but also as farmers. Fulas are unique in West Africa for their Caucasion features: small, slender bodies and sometimes straight, black hair. They are also known for their deep commitment to Islam.

Soninke The Soninke are an old group: the rulers of the Ghana empire were Soninke. The Soninke make up only about 7 percent of the country's population. They are good businessmen. In Gambia, they are often the middlemen: they buy and sell goods, cattle, and real estate. Many are also in the construction business.

Aku The Aku or Creoles are descendants of liberated slaves from the Caribbean. Because they are actually from many different parts of Africa, there is no physical feature that distinguishes them, although most wear Western clothes and are Christians. Akus do not generally intermarry with other Gambians. They speak the local languages and also speak their own brand of pidgin English, using such words as "humbug," "cutlass," "yonder," and "I de go come" (meaning, "I am going and will come back"). Akus are of-

ten market women, farmers, clerks, and government officials. The majority of the doctors in the country are Akus.

Other groups There are also other groups in Gambia, but they are small in number: Sedede, Hausa from Nigeria, and Mandingos from Portuguese Guinea. About five hundred foreigners live in Gambia, including a large number of British, most of whom work in the government; about sixty Americans, mostly Peace Corps Volunteers; several hundred Lebanese shopkeepers and businessmen, some of whom have Gambian citizenship; East Indian businessmen; Senegalese; Ghanaians; Mauritanians; and Swedes.

HOLIDAYS

Four times during each year, Gambia is in a festive mood. The two important religious holidays for Muslims are the end of Ramadan (the month when Muslims fast during the day) and Tabaski (the celebration of God's release of Abraham.) To test his faith, God told Abraham to sacrifice his son Isaac, then had compassion on Abraham and let him sacrifice a sheep instead. On Tabaski, Muslims, dressed in their best clothes, flock to the mosque to pray together. When the prayers are finished, the *imam,* or prayer leader, washes and then slaughters a sheep. This is the signal for each family to go home and kill a sheep or goat. It is customary to give pieces of meat away and also to cook an

A Peace Corps worker teaches apprentice mechanics.

especially fine dinner to which guests are invited. Before and after dinner, people stroll around, chatting with friends. Another festive day is Independence Day, February 18. This is a day of parades, speeches, bands, drumming, and official receptions.

Although the great majority of Gambians are Muslims, Christmas is nonetheless a holiday time, but not a religious holiday. Many years ago, the Portuguese introduced *fanals,* lighted paper lanterns, to Gambia. During the Christmas season, delicate designs are cut out of the fanal by skilled craftsmen—usually older boys. Each fanal is carried through the streets, accompanied by the club that sponsors the lantern. The fanal stops at each compound for people to donate money to the club. The fanals are then judged. When Christmas is over, the fanals are carried to their owners, who claim them amidst dancing and drumming.

Kankorang, or Mumbo Jumbo, also displays himself during Christmas. Kankorang is a man covered in tree bark, who dances and scares children by shaking, twisting, and jumping.

A native orchestra plays for a celebration.

A fishing village on the banks of the river.

THE WAY OF LIFE

Although Gambia's official language is English, most Gambians speak their tribal tongue. Radio programs are usually broadcast in different local languages.

In the countryside, life is basically the same as it has been for centuries. The urban areas, however, are drawing more and more young people away from the small villages. Many youth are dissatisfied with life in the villages but are too unskilled to find jobs in the towns. Many want to work for the government, but there are not enough jobs for all. The government plans to open more technical schools and promote modern agricultural techniques.

HEALTH

Another problem is health. Malaria is still widespread, and babies often die from this mosquito-carried disease. The British have long supported a Medical Research

THE GAMBIA

Above: These men are working on the preparation of a vaccine. Below: The Royal Victorian Hospital in Banjul.

MICHAEL ROBERTS

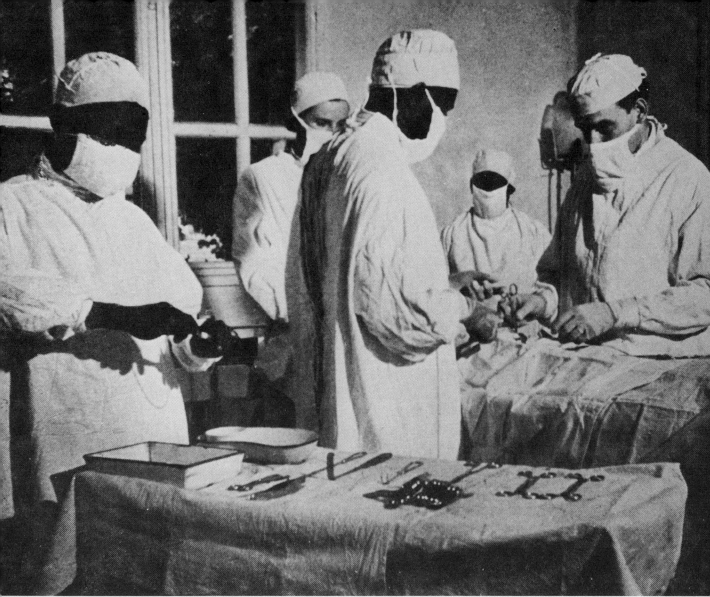

An operation in progress at Bansang Hospital.

Center here, which is trying to develop a vaccine that will give at least six months' immunity.

Gambia has one of the best health systems in West Africa. The main government hospital is in Banjul. Scattered throughout the country are government health clinics run by trained medical staffs. There are two hospitals upriver, a government hospital in Bansang, and a clinic hospital staffed by Germans in Basse Santa Su.

The People Work in The Gambia

Although there is unemployment in Gambia, there is no real poverty. There are no beggars, and few people ever go to bed hungry. But people sometimes say they have not eaten all day. What they mean is that they have not eaten *rice,* though they have probably eaten fruit, vegetables, and game or fish. Gambians grow some subsistence crops—rice, sorghum, corn, cassava, and beans—but not enough to feed the country. Usually during the rainy season before the harvest, there is no rice left from the previous year's crop, so people must then rely on other foods.

Gambia hopes to become self-sufficient in rice production. Nationalist Chinese have been teaching Gambians how to grow rice in irrigated lands, rather than with the

New construction along the river near Banjul.

dry techniques most Gambians have been using. The Nationalist Chinese have concentrated their efforts on MacCarthy Island and in the Sapu Swamps, as these areas show promise of producing enough rice to have a surplus for export. The fertility of the land and the availability of fresh water from the Gambia River makes these areas target ones for production. With new irrigation methods, the rice crop can be almost tripled.

Most farmers in Gambia plant peanuts, which make up 95 percent of the country's exports. Exports are raw peanuts or refined peanut oil. If Gambia has a poor peanut crop, the whole country suffers: parents cannot pay their children's school fees, farmers cannot afford imported rice when their own supplies run out, and the

Above: Bagging peanuts at a collection center of a farmer's cooperation produce union.
Below: Preparing peanuts to be shipped for export.

Much of Gambia's rice is grown in swamps that were originally covered with mangrove trees. Above: Workers cultivate rice. Right: Rice being harvested. The mangroves can be seen in the background. Below: An Indian rice specialist demonstrates the method of sun drying rice seeds.

Tourists arriving in Gambia.

people cannot afford meat or onions and tomato paste for their soup. During the last few years, peanuts have produced a high yield and prices have been high.

Fortunately for Gambia, two industries—tourism and fishing—are blossoming. It appears that in the future there will be less dependence on peanuts for the country's economy.

During the planting time before the rains start, "strange farmers" (as they are called by Gambians) come from Mali, Senegal, and Guinea to help the farmers. This has been going on for hundreds of years. A "strange farmer" works for a Gambian farmer three days, farms for himself on the land the farmer lends him, and gets free housing in return. He lives on the land until harvest time, which comes after the rains.

TOURISM

The tourist industry recently exploded in Gambia. There were no tourists in 1965, except for occasional stray adventurers, and there were only two tourist-class hotels. Then a Swedish woman visited Gambia, settled there, and opened a radio station. She began telling other Swedes about the country. Because Gambia's winter climate is perfect for Europeans, many Swedes began to visit. The Gambian government was interested in tourists and promised a five-year tax exemption to tour operators and hotel owners.

At first, a jetload of Scandinavians came every other week. Then two more hotels were built, and soon a jetload of tourists came every week. More hotels were built

A new luxury tourist hotel in Banjul.

by Scandinavians, British, and the Gambian government. Two Swedish tour companies organized groups, and in 1971-72 British tourists started coming. More hotels were built, several with swimming pools. Thousands of tourists come on charter flights and on cruise ships each year.

The tourist industry has directly employed thirty-five hundred Gambians, mostly young dropouts who would otherwise be unemployed. Before each season, hotel schools train workers in restaurant and hotel management. Receptionists are sent to Sweden to learn Swedish and take courses in accounting and typing. Each

year, forty of the most promising workers are sent to Germany to learn hotel and restaurant management. The Gambian government hopes that the best of these people will eventually be in charge of Gambia's hotels.

Not only has tourism benefited Gambians working in the hotels; others have done well, too. An egg farm has expanded and new farms are being started. More vegetables are being raised, and hotels are buying local meat instead of importing it. A large tourist market has opened and is flourishing. Locally dyed batik and tie-dyed cloth is very popular. Several Gam-

Gambian dancers, both traditional and modern, have become popular with tourists.

Poultry farms, like the one above, have expanded because of the increase of tourists.

bian women have done so well that they now support all their relatives, have built nice homes, and have made trips to Mecca. The many tailors in Banjul have to work overtime in order to finish all the shirts, dresses, and hats ordered by tourists. Traditional dance groups and rock groups are hired by the hotels, children hire themselves out as guides, wood carvers are busy making masks, goldsmiths are hiring assistants to help them make more jewelry, and leatherworkers are making purses and sandals. Taxi owners, too, are making more money.

Such a boom has been bad in some ways.

High school and junior secondary school students have quit school to become guides, and petty thievery has increased. Some Gambians resent tourists taking their pictures, dancing with their daughters, and walking on their beaches. Hunting by tourists has ceased while the government checks to see how much wildlife remains. How many tourists the country can hold remains to be seen, but Gambia is calling on experts to help them. The experts have even devised tax schedules to make sure Gambia receives its share of the tourist dollar. Gambian officials are making trips to other tourist-oriented coun-

Above: Children play in the river near the fishing boats. Below: Nets are used to catch many kinds of fish. Here the nets are hanging out to dry.

MICHAEL ROBERTS

Fresh smoked oysters are sold in the market and along the main highway.

tries to see how other people handle the same problems.

FISHING

The fishing industry is not as well developed as is tourism. In 1972 fifteen hundred tons of fish were exported. Because Gambia is rich in seafood, other countries are becoming interested in this area. Ghanaian and Senegalese fishermen live and fish along the coast, Chinese come to buy dried shark, and Japanese have opened a gigantic quick-freeze factory and are exporting shrimp, lobster, and many varieties of fish to Europe and Japan. The Japanese outfit more than one hundred local boats and four large Japanese trawlers.

Ghanaians and Gambians have constructed long, thatched buildings in Gunjur, and other villages, where they smoke bonga fish for local use and for export to Sierra Leone and Ghana. Many fishermen along the river sell to the local people and each village has its own fisherman.

On the estuaries, Jola women collect oysters from the mangrove roots and small clams from tidal mud flats; they smoke them and sell them in the market and along the main highway.

Gambian fishing boats are very narrow and not more than fifteen feet long. In these delicate boats, with hand lines and nets, fishermen land two-hundred-pound, eight-foot-long sharks.

ANIMAL RAISING

There are more cattle and goats in Gambia than people. Experts say that the country is overgrazed. For many years, Mandingo and Fula cattle owners kept their cattle as wealth, hoarding rather than selling them. The cattle were a part of the bride price. At the same time, the butchers in Banjul had a strong union that kept the price paid to the cattle owners at a minimum. This did nothing to stimulate sale by traditional herders.

The government has now set up a feed lot and is controlling the butchering. The government has regulated the price paid to cattle owners and designated an information campaign supporting the selection of weak and older cattle from the herds and the improvement of breeding practices. With controlled higher prices, the cattle owners are beginning to see the value of raising and selling their cattle for a profit. The government is also encouraging the export of beef to other West African countries.

OTHER INDUSTRIES

Gambia still has far to go to balance its trade; that is, to export the same amount

There are more goats and cattle in Gambia than people. Goats are very useful and have been called the poor man's cow. A goat is a grass eater and a relative of a sheep. It is usefull for its milk, flesh, hair, and hide.

A Gambian policeman uses an imported bicycle.

that it imports. Other exports besides peanuts and fish include tie-dyed cloth, palm kernels, beeswax, beef, hides, and skins. Some goods that are imported, such as tomato paste (which every Gambian family uses almost daily), could be produced in Gambia. Other imports, such as hardware, radios, and bicycles must be imported.

With few exceptions, all imports are handled by foreigners. There are Lebanese, Moroccan, Mauritanian, East Indian, French, and British shops with imported goods. Foreigners even own the car agencies, garages, and gasoline stations.

The hundreds of tiny, closet-sized shops throughout Gambia, where sugar, tea, soft drinks, pencils, cloth, and thread can be bought, are often run by Mauritanians and Lebanese. Gambians have small shops in the marketplace.

Most of the clothing is made in the country. Gambians grow cotton, out of which cotton cloth is woven and dyed. Traditional weavers have made this coarse but beautiful material in long, narrow strips for at least eight hundred years. But cotton cloth is too expensive and fine for most Gambians' everyday wear. Gambians import unprinted grey cotton and tie-dye or batik it, at which point it can be exported. All types of cloth are available in Gambia—from expensive velvet and Swiss lace to cheaper Indian, Eastern European, and Asian cloth.

78

Shops close for a few hours during the warm afternoons.

Right: Many kinds of clothes are sold in the market, from everyday wear to dress for festive occasions. Below: Young children, like these boys, help sell produce at the market.

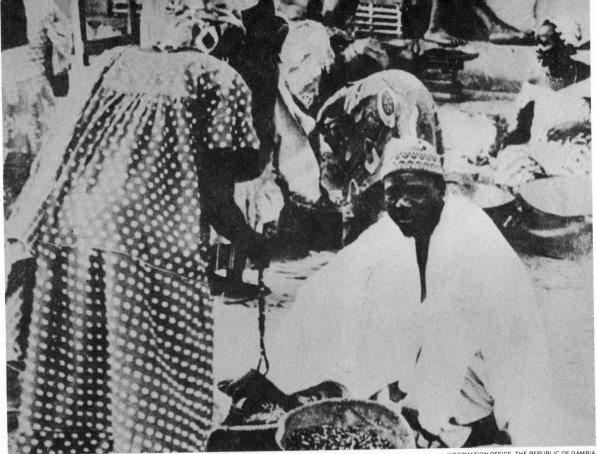

A woman shopping in the market at Kuntaur.

There is hardly a street in the towns or a road in the villages without a tailor, and every marketplace has tailors as well. Gambian tailors—all men—are skillful and can make a shirt in one day. Most Gambian shirts and blouses are embroidered. On festive occasions, heavily embroidered *caftans* (ankle-length garments with long sleeves), shirts, and dresses are worn. In the past, shirts and caftans were embroidered by hand; today they are all machine-sewn. Many tailors have expensive treadle or electric sewing machines with embroidery attachments.

But the best embroidery is done by some expensive three-needle machines.

Other industries in Gambia include a soft drink bottling plant and a factory that makes plastic sandals. Gambians have begun making grass and raffia furniture for the hotels.

At present, Gambia has no mineral industry. Ilmenite, an important ore source of titanium, is found in veins, leach sands, and river placers. But this ore has proved to be expensive to mine. The only other known mineral of possible commercial value is kaolin, which is the clay used to

On some days the market is very crowded.

82

make pottery. Kaolin deposits near Basse Santa Su will soon be developed for export of this mineral.

THE MARKETPLACE

Every village has a marketplace; the bigger towns of Banjul, Brikama, Serrekunda, Bassa Santa Su, and Georgetown have large markets. The market is really the center of town, where local products are bought and sold, where everyone meets to gossip, and where people smoke and play *drafts,* checkers. Merchants sit at the same place every day, scrubbing their vegetables and fruits and placing them in neat mounds in front of them. Bargaining goes on while radios play, children nurse, and women call to each other. Depending on the season, papayas, mangoes, tomatoes, cabbage, lettuce, hot peppers, peanuts, peanut butter, squash, beans, "bitter" tomatoes, potatoes, onions, kola nuts, and delicacies such as fufu and peanut brittle are sold. In another part of the market, butchers sell beef, lamb, and fish. Brightly colored pots from the USSR and other Eastern European countries are sold in yet another section. Sellers call out to the buyers in English, Wolof, or Mandingo: "Come see my good things today. I have fine prices." Sometimes the buyer is pushed and pulled as merchants vie to sell their goods.

The Enchantment of The Gambia

Gambians were surprised when their country recently became so popular with tourists. There are thirty-five miles of sandy beaches—a magnet even to Gambians, who visit there with friends, strolling, fishing, and playing, while children swim in the waves and quiet tidal pools. The ocean is calm—without the undertow of the countries to the south and without the rocks of northern Senegal. In some areas palm trees line the beaches. One can walk for miles without seeing anyone. At a beachside village, fishermen bring in catches from their painted canoes.

Birdwatchers come from all over the world to take notes on the hovering jalango, take pictures of the turquoise Senegal kingfisher, or watch the pelican fill his bill with fish. Special paths especially for birdwatchers are presently being constructed.

Fifteen miles south of Banjul, a large nature reserve has been carefully created out of a natural swamp area. The area is quite safe, but a visitor must watch out that a friendly red calabas monkey does not jump down on him from a tree branch. Snakes, deer, crocodile, and wild birds can be seen.

Fishermen can go deep-sea fishing in boats, but swordfish, shark, and smaller fish can be caught right on the old bridge connecting Banjul with the mainland. That is where everyone—Lebanese merchants, peanut farmers, and ambassadors—meet to fish and tell fish stories. Surf fishing is excellent all along the coast.

Visitors are always fascinated by the

The sandy beaches along the Atlantic shore are very popular with tourists.

INFORMATION OFFICE. THE REPUBLIC OF GAMBIA

Above: Large decorated canoes are used to transport crops on the river. Below: The port at Banjul is crowded with large freighters when peanuts are being shipped.

Oceangoing vessels can navigate the Gambia River for 150 miles to Kuntaur and smaller steamers can go 50 miles farther.

river and the life that surrounds it. In the Banjul harbor, porpoises jump out of the water. Along the river, troops of monkeys and baboons pay little attention to human beings. Hippopotamuses live in the river, but they are rarely seen; at the slightest sound, they sink underneath the surface of the water.

When the *Lady Wright,* the government mail boat, makes its way upriver, whole communities, curious to see what the boat is bringing to their village, come to the river bank to wave and call out to friends. The boat carries traders with chickens, kola nuts, salt, and cloth; cattle, goats, and cooking pots; mail; tourists; and students returning from Banjul to their villages.

Banjul's waterfront is lined with heavy, colonnaded old buildings. This is where large Lebanese shops are found, which carry everything from cloth and toys to brass pots from the Middle East. Here stands the President's Mansion, built before independence. Once the home of the British governors, it was built high up to catch the ocean breezes. It has high ceilings, verandas, and lovely gardens.

There is always drumming and dancing

going on in and around Banjul. It might be a Jola wedding dance or maybe a Hausa dance—where a costumed male dancer and assistant run after boys, scaring them with a stick. Gambian women love dancing and beautiful cloth. If a visitor is fortunate enough to be in Banjul on a big occasion, he will see the fine cloth and excellent dancing. Some women count their wealth in cloth and jewels. The wife of an important man might have cloth that sells for forty or fifty dollars a yard. Some gold earrings are so heavy they have to be supported with strings tied around the head.

On Tabaski Day, the grandest holiday of the year, men stroll the streets in wide-waisted pants and tunics and caftans embroidered in gold or silver threads. They wear hats and shoes made out of velvet and embroidered with gold.

There are many historic sites to be explored in Gambia. Perhaps the most fascinating are the fort at Barra, the slave prison at Georgetown, and the ancient stone circles at different sites upriver.

Though Gambia is naturally beautiful, perhaps its most important feature is that the people, from differing groups with different customs, are able to live peacefully together.

People have always come to Gambia because it offered them a chance to live well. They have followed the Wolof Saying: "Live in the country which offers you the best opportunity for life-fulfillment."

Alex Haley, a black American, spent twelve years tracing his family tree. He discovered that he was descended from a Gambian slave, Kunta Kinte, who was captured in the eighteenth century and sold to a Virginia planter. This account is told in the book, "Roots," which was made into an eight-part television series.

An aerial view of Banjul.

Handy Reference Section

Political:

Official Name—Republic of The Gambia

Capital—Banjul

Monetary Unit—Dalasi (one Dalasi=1/5 of a British pound sterling, or about US $.50)

Official Language—English

National Flag—Three wide, horizontal strips (from top to bottom: red, blue, and green) are separated by two narrow, white stripes. Red represents the sun, blue represents the river, green represents agricultural resources, and white represents unity and peace.

Symbol—Two lions supporting and protecting a crest of a palm and a knight's helmet. The lions are also holding traditional farming implements: a hoe and an ax.

National Motto—"Progress, Peace, Prosperity"

Geographical:

Area—4004 square miles (excluding the river)

Length—Approximately 202 miles

Greatest Width—Approximately 40 miles

Narrowest Width—Approximately 9 miles

POPULATION

Population—494,000 (1973 estimate)

Population Density—123 people per square mile

Population Growth Rate—2.1 percent per year

Birth Rate per 1000—42.5

Life Expectancy (after first year)—41.0 years

Infant Mortality (per 1000 live births)—82.6

PRINCIPAL CITIES

Banjul	39,476
Serrekunda	25,505
Brikama	9,483
Basse Santa Su	2,899
Georgetown	2,510

GOVERNMENTAL DIVISIONS

Divisions	*Headquarters*
Western	Brikama
Lower River	Kerewan
MacCarthy Island	Georgetown
Upper River	Basse Santa Su

NATIONAL DAYS

Independence Day—February 18
Idal Fitr—End of Ramadan (Muslim month of fasting) (moveable)
Tabaski—Muslim holiday (moveable)
Christmas Day—December 25

YOU HAVE A DATE WITH HISTORY

1000 A.D.—High point of Ghana empire

1240—Sundiata defeats remainder of Ghana empire, forms Mali empire

1250s—Sundiata sends Tiramang to conquer land south of Gambia River

1455—Prince Henry of Portugal sends Alvise Cadamosto to explore Gambia

1512—Many small kingdoms founded in Gambia; Koli leads Fula into Gambia

1618—First British traders enter Gambia River; slave trading multiplies

1667—Slaves on James Island rebel

1700s—Time of greatest slave trading; Gambian mansas remain independent; many Gambians become Muslims

1783—Gambia awarded to Britain in Treaty of Versailles

1807—British government abolishes slave trading; Gambia officially named a British Settlement

1816—British begin colonizing by purchasing Banjul Island

1821—First Christian schools established by missionaries

1831—Freed slaves from British colonies in New World sent to Gambia; Kementang resists British at Georgetown on MacCarthy Island; mansa of Barra attacks British on Barra Point

1834—Kementang again attacks MacCarthy Island

1843—Gambia chartered as separate colony

c. 1848—Peanut exportation begins

1850—Beginning of Muslim religious battles against Soninke chiefs

1866-88—Gambia administered by British in Sierra Leone

1868—End of Soninke domination of area of Gambia and Senegal south of Gambia River

1873—Fodi Silah and Fodi Kabba expand religious war, attacking British domination

1889—France and England determine boundaries between Gambia and Senegal

c. 1902—Gambia divided into provinces; Gambians lose their independence to the British

1923—Small starts first Gambian newspaper

1929—Small founds Bathurst Trade Union

1954—First Gambians allowed in legislative council

1963—Britain grants Gambia full internal self-government; Njie elected first Gambian chief minister

1964—D. K. Jawara becomes prime minister

1965—Gambia achieves full independence as constitutional monarchy; Gambia becomes member of UN

1970—Gambia becomes a republic; Jawara elected president

Index

About the Authors

With the publication of his first book for school use when he was twenty, **Allan Carpenter** began a career as an author that has spanned more than 135 books—with more still to be published in the Enchantment of Africa series for Childrens Press. After teaching in the public schools of Des Moines, Mr. Carpenter began his career as an educational publisher at the age of twenty-one when he founded the magazine *Teachers Digest.* In the field of educational periodicals, he was responsible for many innovations. During his many years in publishing, he has perfected a highly organized approach to handling large volumes of factual material: after extensive traveling and having collected all possible materials, he systematically reviews and organizes everything. From his apartment high in Chicago's John Hancock Building, Allan recalls: "My collection and assimilation of materials on the states and countries began before the publication of my first book." Allan is the founder of Carpenter Publishing House and of Infordata International, Inc., publishers of *Issues in Education* and *Index to U.S. Government Periodicals.* When he is not writing or traveling, his principal avocation is music. He has been the principal bassist of many symphonies, and he managed the country's leading non-professional symphony for twenty-five years.

Susan and **Loyd Kepferle** have spent seven years with the Peace Corps in Africa and South America. They lived two and one-half years in The Gambia, both in urban Banjul and rural Cape St. Mary's close to the ocean. As Peace Corps Director, Loyd spent much of his time developing Peace Corps projects throughout the country with Gambians from different areas of the country as well as Peace Corps volunteers. Although presently living in Boise, Idaho, where Loyd is a specialist in rural health and Susan teaches English as a second language, the Kepferles definitely plan to return with their three children to their favorite West African country, The Gambia.